ESSENTIAL ELEMENTS®

GUITAR ENSEMBLES

J.S. BACH

T0065951

CONTENTS

Arrangements by Mark Phillips

ISBN 978-1-4803-6045-7

HAL•LEONARD®
CORPORATION
7777 W. BLUEMOUND RD. P.O. BOX 13819 MILWAUKEE, WI 53213

In Australia Contact:
Hal Leonard Australia Pty. Ltd.
4 Lentara Court
Cheltenham, Victoria, 3192 Australia
Email: ausadmin@halleonard.com.au

Visit Hal Leonard Online at
www.halleonard.com

AIR ON THE G STRING

from ORCHESTRAL SUITE NO. 3

By Johann Sebastian Bach

ARIOSO

By Johann Sebastian Bach

BE THOU WITH ME

By Johann Sebastian Bach

BOURRÉE IN E MINOR

By Johann Sebastian Bach

Moderately fast

GAVOTTE
from FRENCH SUITE NO. 5
By Johann Sebastian Bach

JESU, JOY OF MAN'S DESIRING

By Johann Sebastian Bach

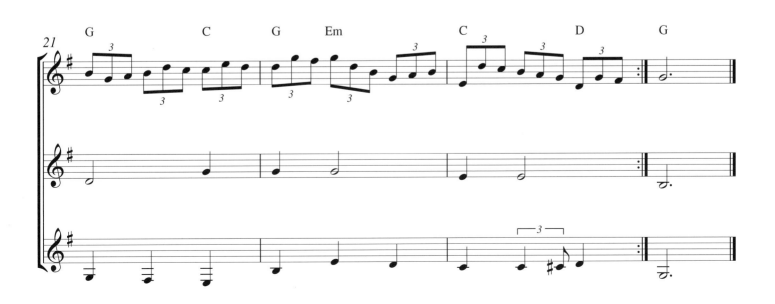

KEEP, O MY SPIRIT

from CHRISTMAS ORATORIO

By Johann Sebastian Bach

MARCH IN D MAJOR
from the LITTLE CLAVIER BOOK FOR ANNA MAGDALENA BACH
By Johann Sebastian Bach

MINUET IN G MAJOR
from the ANNA MAGDALENA NOTEBOOK
By Johann Sebastian Bach

MINUET IN G MINOR
BWV Anh. 115
By Johann Sebastian Bach

MUSETTE IN D MAJOR

from the LITTLE CLAVIER BOOK FOR ANNA MAGDALENA BACH

By Johann Sebastian Bach

SHEEP MAY SAFELY GRAZE
from CANTATA NO. 208

By Johann Sebastian Bach

SICILIANO
from SONATA NO. 2 FOR HARPSICHORD AND FLUTE
By Johann Sebastian Bach

SLEEPERS, AWAKE (WACHET AUF)

from CANTATA NO. 140

By Johann Sebastian Bach